COSMOPOLITAN

Love Letters

COSMOPOLITAN
Love Letters

Sheila Kurtz, M.G.A.
and The Graphology Consulting Group

Robson Books

First published in Great Britain in 1996 by Robson Books Ltd, Bolsover House, 5-6 Clipstone Street, London W1P 8LE as *Handwriting Analysis for Lovers*.
This edition published in Great Britain in 1997 by Robson Books Ltd.
Copyright © 1996 Sheila Kurtz and Barney Collier
The right of Sheila Kurtz and Barney Collier to be identified as authors of this work has been asserted by them in accordance with the Copyright, Designs and Patents Act 1988

British Library Cataloguing in Publication Data
A catalogue record for this title is available from the British Library

ISBN: 1 86105 108 5

The expression *Cosmopolitan* is the trademark of The National Magazine Company Limited and The Hearst Corporation, registered in the UK and the USA, and other principal countries of the world, and is the absolute property of The National Magazine Company Limited and The Hearst Corporation. The use of this trademark other than with the express permission of The National Magazine Company or The Hearst Corporation is strictly prohibited.

All rights reserved. No part of this publication may be reproduced, stored in a retrieval system, or transmitted in any form or by any means, electronic, mechanical, photocopying, recording or otherwise, without the prior permission in writing of the publishers.

Printed by The Guernsey Press Company Limited
Guernsey, Channel Islands

THANKS TO

Jackie Meyer, a visionary editor at Warner Books, who created the idea for this book, and her friend Leslie Schnur, editor-in-chief of Dell, who had the imagination to publish it. Harvey Klinger, a good friend and agent, who is always encouraging. Kristin Kiser, our editor, who tested the truthfulness of this book upon her own fiancé.

Love

Love is among the best reasons in the world to analyze a lover's handwriting. While love allows you to see things about your lover that may be obscure to others, you may be reluctant to know more than your senses already tell.

ANALYSIS of your lover's handwriting will present you with a portrait of your lover that is

UNINTOXICATED with *amour,*

UNIMPRESSED by physical beauty,

UNBIASED as to gender, race, or national origin,

PRECISE enough to be of value to forensic scientists,

BROAD enough to encompass 300 traits of personality—and yet

PARTICULAR enough to forecast how compatible you and your lover are likely to be,

IN AND OUT OF THE CLINCHES.

Contents

A Very Brief History of Graphology	1
What You Need to Begin	3
What You Are Looking For	5
To Begin Analysis	11
Thinking Patterns	19
Compatibility	61

A Very Brief History of Graphology

For nearly three centuries, the ruling families of Europe ordered that the handwriting of royal couples about to be engaged be scrutinized by royal graphologists—who would give their opinions on whether the intendeds *actually* were meant for each other.

Graphology has long appeared in the psychology curricula of major universities in Germany, Hungary, France, and Switzerland. In England, investment bankers analyze the handwriting of all new recruits. In France, about 80 percent of the major corporations employ certified handwriting analysts on staff. In Russia and at the Central Intelligence Agency, graphology is used to understand secret agents' personalities better.

Early in the twentieth century, Milton Bunker, a teacher of shorthand, brought the art and science of graphology to the United States. In the last two decades of the century, graphology has grown from a scientific curiosity into a widespread professional practice. Major universities give credits in graphological sciences. Corporations and small businesses use graphology in employment screening and executive compatibility studies.

Today, individuals are finding that graphology is helpful in planning their careers, illuminating their own personal lives, and giving them a winning edge when the ability to read other people accurately really counts.

Love Letters allows many more people to benefit from the clues that graphology can reveal.

What You Need to Begin

A Handwriting Sample

It is best to ask openly for a handwriting sample, particularly if it's from somebody you love.

In the graphology profession, it is unethical, except in forensic work and private investigations, to run graphological analyses on samples obtained surreptitiously.

Handwriting analysis for lovers should be done together. It's a sharing experience. It ought to be aboveboard.

Use **white, unlined paper,** preferably 8 ½ × 11 inches. The use of page space, the alignment of letters, and the slope of lines are individual and indicative. Having lines already on a page interferes with natural expression.

The writing instrument ought to be a **ballpoint pen** because it most accurately transmits pressure to the page.

If the person has writing of average size, the amount of text written should nearly fill the page. If the handwriting is small, half a page is enough.

The content of the sample should not be copied directly from a source. It should be thoughts flowing currently from the writer's mind.

The sample should be written with the writer in a comfortable position at a desk or table. Sign the sample.

If you are working together, your two handwriting samples ought to be examined side by side.

Tools Required

- Three No. 2 pencils, well sharpened
- **Magnifying glass or "loupe"**
- Small protractor (optional)
- **Straightedge**
- Notebook to describe your findings
- Bright light source (A light box is ideal.)
- This book

What You Are Looking For

Graphology is the study of the strokes of handwriting.

This includes the **dots** over *i*s and *j*s; the **bars** on the *t*s; the upper and lower **loops** in many letters; the **tops** of *m*s and *n*s; the beginning and ending hooks on many letters; **flourishes, slant, pressure, clarity** or **muddiness, size, steadiness** or lack of it, and the **spacing** between letters and lines.

How different—and how revealing—handwriting strokes can be

These are *i* dots, *j* dots, circular dots, slashes, wandering dots, close dots, and dots with hooks.

These are *t* bars placed before the stem, over the stem, low on stem, midstem, high-flying, missing, perched to left and right of stem.

These are the upper loops of *h*s, *l*s, *t*s, *d*s, and *k*s.

These are the lower loops of *y*s, *g*s, *p*s, and *j*s.

These are the tops of *m*s and *n*s.

These are the beginning and ending hooks.

Get the True Angle

If you are using this book together, get familiar with both of your side-by-side samples. Acquaint your eye with various graphological strokes by comparing the letter strokes closely with the strokes illustrated on pages 6 and 7. You may find several of them are quite similar or some clearly different. We will discuss out-of-the-ordinary strokes later.

Now, with a straightedge, draw a horizontal line under several lines of writing to establish a *baseline* against which the slant of the words and letters will be measured.

Isak Dinesen's beloved Kamante. I drawings was like touching a talisman had disappeared forever.

Now, with a protractor or just your eye, determine the average angle of the writings.
Choose from:

- **Straight up and down,** where most of the letters and words are drawn at a close-to-90° angle to the baseline.
- **Slanted left** at angles of more than 90°.

- **Slanted right** at angles of less than 90°.

[handwritten signature: Costello Im a Bad Boy]

TIP: Without a straightedge and protractor, it is still possible to make a quick and accurate guess about the slant of handwriting after eyeball-measuring several lines.

To Begin Analysis

Now that you've determined the slant of the writing, it is time to begin your analyses. Take the notebook you are using to describe your findings and draw a line down the middle of several pages. One side is for your handwriting, the other for that of your lover or other significant person.

Slant

The slant of handwriting expresses the intense mental feelings of the individual and indicates how these feelings are controlled.

Take note of the particular handwriting slant in the proper column in your notebook, and record your findings after reading the following clues.

CLUES

Straight up-and-down handwriting is a clue to a personality that keeps emotions under average control. This usually means that emotions do not overly color studied judgments. Feelings of emotion—joy, fear, humiliation, exaltation, and others—take second place to thinking.

Handwriting that **slants to the left** indicates a higher level of introspection than at the vertical. Such a person maintains tight control over emotional expression and may appear to some as cold and rigid. In interpersonal communications, such a person may seem remote and difficult to fathom.

The **farther to the left** the writing slants, the more introverted the writer is and the more lacking in the trust that permits satisfying intimacy. There is also increased difficulty in verbal person-to-person communications, although written, artistic, and theatrical communications may be a successful outlet for emotional expression. The handwriting styles of Jacqueline Kennedy Onassis and President Ronald Reagan both have left-leaning slants, which are characteristic of people who keep their emotions reined.

If the slant is **slightly or moderately to the right** (more than 45°), the writer may express more vivacity and verve than the vertical writer. Right-slanting writers can show and talk about their emotions without excessive guardedness or inhibition.

If the slant is **decidedly to the right** (less than 45°), the "heart rules the mind." This type of person may be impulsive, socially aggressive (sometimes called "outgoing"), and may have loud hysterics and act out strong emotions intensely. The farther the slant leans right, the higher the likelihood of inappropriately uncontrolled behavior. Former Vice President Dan Quayle's handwriting leans far over to the right.

In handwriting with a **variable slant,** the letters slant in more than one direction. Straight up and down and to the right or left is not uncommon. This multiple slant indicates **versatility** and **adaptability** in new situations with **flexible perspectives**.

In handwriting with an **erratic slant,** the letters vary from 0° to 180° with no apparent rhyme or reason. An erratic slant is a clue to **lack of reliability** in most aspects of life.

Pressure

Next you must determine handwriting **pressure**, which is how firmly or gently the writer wields the writing instruments. To do so, feel the paper upon which the samples are written. Then answer the following questions.

1. Can you feel the rib made by the pen point on the opposite side of the page? If so, this indicates **heavy pressure**. *(Paper torn because of excessive pen pressure indicates a person overwrought with tension.)*
2. Are there no ribs on the back of the page, and is the writing dark enough to be easily readable? If so, this indicates **moderate pressure,** which is what most people apply.
3. Does the writing appear clear yet float lightly on the surface of the paper? If so, this indicates **light pressure**, found in the

writing of about 10 percent of the population.

Indicate the correct pressures in your notes, and follow this with a notation of the appropriate clues.

CLUES

Heavy pressure indicates the writer is physically and mentally **overagitated by stressful situations.** The writer may be highly excited by appetites and desires. Feelings may be exaggerated and energy expenditures may be above normal. Thomas Alva Edison used energetic pressure in his writing.

People who use **moderate pressure** cope with life's stressful situations in **balanced** ways and without long, lingering anxiousness.

Stress hardly bothers people who use **light pressure.** They cope neatly with life's business, and **few situations "bother" them.** Extremely light pressure indicates minimal energy expenditure is a way of life.

Size

In most situations, handwriting from 1 to 7 points is **small**.

Now is the time for all good men to come to the aid of the party.

From 8 to 19 points is **middling**.

Now is the time for all good Men to

From 20 to 48 points is **large**.

Dear Mr and Mrs Mrs Kaig and El

Make your notations about size in the appropriate columns in your notebook based on the following clues.

CLUES

Small writing indicates an **ability to concentrate and focus mental energy** and pay **attention to details**. The intensity required to write so small tends to rub off on all other traits.

Medium is the size most of us write.

Large writing indicates an **urge toward expansiveness** in some area, including a **desire for space, for attention,** and **theatricality.** With an equally large signature, large writing is a sign of **exaggerated self-worth.**

Clarity vs. Muddiness

Look at the samples and record appropriate clues.

CLUES

Are the circle letters, such as the *a* and the *o*, muddied with ink?

If so, there is room for concern. Muddy writing indicates the possibility of **excessive appetites:**

drugs or food or **addictions;** other medical problems.

Thinking Patterns

From this point on, you will see illustrations of particular handwriting characteristics and be asked to notice and record similarities to the handwriting in your samples.

In your notebook, record the appropriate clues in the appropriate columns.

Look at the letters *m* and *n* in the handwriting samples.

Is there a visible V-shaped formation in these letters?

If so, the V-shape indicates **analytical skills.** The larger and deeper the V-shape, the more likely the writer will seek his or her own information and separate it into its parts for examination and interpretation. Malcolm Forbes, the late publisher of *Forbes* magazine, had pronounced v formations in his script.

Are the tops of the *m*s and *n*s rounded?

m n M N

If so, the writer is a **methodical and logical** thinker building fact upon fact to reach conclusions. This is a cumulative process that requires enough time to gather facts, sift and sort them, and then reach conclusions. Such people may try the patience of faster thinkers. **Intuition** will speed up this thinking process.

Do the tops of the *m*s and *n*s form wedges or mountain peaks?

m n M N

If so, the writer is **investigative** by nature, in search of new findings and discoveries, delving **curiously** into the unknown. The late Lorne Greene, the actor, scripted wedges and peaks.

Do the tops of the *m*s and *n*s have needle points?

If so, the writer **picks up new information very quickly** and understands new concepts without long explanations. He or she is a **comprehensive thinker** with the ability to retrieve information rapidly from memory.

Are the *m*s and *n*s scrawled without much definition?

If so, the writer relies solely upon the data at hand and doesn't probe below the surface. This can be a sign of **weak or weakened thinking.** President Richard Nixon scripted nearly needle-point *m*s and *n*s at the beginning of his career. At the end, his *m*s and *n*s were nothing but a long, nearly flat line.

[signature] 1968

[signature] EARLY 1974

[signature] LATE 1974

Look at all the letters in your writing samples and closely examine how they are connected.

Are there separations between letters within words?

When in The course of human events, our fore- fathers brought to This

If so, there is an indication of **intuitive ability**. The writer can leap over gaps in data to reach conclusions. This is a nonlogical form of thinking that cannot be justified using typical forms of logic. Nevertheless, the conclusions can be accurate, and intuitive thinking is common to "genius." Intuition accelerates every thinking process.

Imagination

Look at the **lower loops** in the letters *y, g,* and *j.*

Are the loops large and full?

If so, the writer possesses an ability to create **original ideas** in virtually any area. If the loops are disproportionately large, the ideas may be overblown and unrealistic.

Are the lower loops nonexistent?

If so, the person is likely to be **a loner** who prefers working in a solitary situation, someone who seldom enjoys crowds or large parties. Humphrey Bogart, the actor, had no lower loops at all.

Are the lower loops narrow and constricted?

If so, the writer is **extremely selective** in the people with whom he or she associates. Usually people with similar ideas and values are chosen.

Are there relatively long lower loops in the *y, g,* or *j?*

If so, the writer **needs change and variety.** Routine tends to stifle the imagination of these people, and structured settings bore them. They often **enjoy travel** for the new people and new vistas it provides. Senator Orin Hatch, Republican from Utah, has long lower loops.

Are the upper loops of the *l, h,* and *b* full?

ℓ h b

If so, the writer has tendencies toward **religious, philosophical,** and **spiritual thinking.**

Are there upper loops with inverted V-shaped formations at the tops?

If so, the writer is exploring philosophical and spiritual ideas but is **still in the questioning stage.**

Are the upper loops quite short, rising just above the mundane level of the rest of the writing?

hotel California, you check in, not out.

If so, this indicates **a practical bent** that limits exploration of the mystical and unknown.

Goals

Goals are preset mental objectives toward which a person may strive with varying directness and speed.

Look at the bar that crosses (or doesn't cross) the *stem* of the *t*.

Does the *t* bar fly over the *t* stem without touching it?

If so, the writer has **visionary goals.** Such people are dreamers. Their goals are **usually too high to reach in reality.** These people tend to live in fantasy worlds, and they don't know it.

Are the *t* bars sitting on the top of the *t* stem, just touching it?

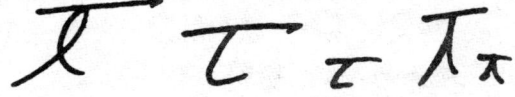

If so, the writer has very **ambitious goals** with many things to achieve in present and future. **Visions are realistic.**

Are the *t* bars placed in the center of the stem?

If so, goals are **neither too high nor too low** and are set so as to be easily attainable. Actress Brooke Shields has centered *t* bars.

Is the *t* bar placed near the bottom of the stem?

Few goals are set by this writer, who **often underestimates his or her own ability** and thus is reluctant to set objectives for fear of failing to reach them. People who write this way are capable of short-term projects and affairs.

Are the *t* bars higher at the ends than in the middle?

If so, the writer has little interest in setting objectives and **"takes life as it comes."** He or she has little interest in assuming long-term commitments. This formation is seldom seen in the writing of well-known and successful people.

Achievement

Achievement is the accomplishment of objectives and aspirations set by oneself or others.

Look at all the **lowercase** *f*s and *t*s in the sample.

Are there "tie" strokes—strokes that go to the left, then tie through the letter on their way to the right?

If so, the writer is **persistent** and will keep on going in spite of obstacles. The more tie strokes in the sample, the more persistence is indicated. When tie strokes are found in the *t* bars (*see illustration*), the trait of persistence is even stronger because it involves willpower.

Look at the final strokes of the *t*s in the sample. Is there an upward and outward "breakaway" swing of the strokes away from a preceding stroke above the baseline?

If so, the writer shows **initiative.** When an opportunity is seen, decisive steps are taken to pursue it, without anyone else's urging. The breakaway stroke can be found in other letters, although its strongest manifestation is in the final *t*.

Look at the strokes of the *g*s, *y*s, and *j*s that fall below the baseline of the writing sample.

Is there a strong forward swing of the upstroke away from the downstroke of a letter below the baseline?

young

If so, the writer exhibits an action trait that indicates a **driving energy** in pursuit of a goal. There is usually increased pressure in the stroke when it goes up toward the baseline. This is seen in successful salespeople and politicians, former Vice President Dan Quayle among them.

Look at the stems of the *t*s and *d*s in the sample. (Ignore the *t* bar.)
Are the stems approximately twice as tall as the other lowercase letters?

test it out

If so, the writer has considerable **self-respect.** Approval from others is desired and becomes a basis for judging one's self-worth.

Look at all the small *f*s in the sample.

Are the top and bottom halves of the *f*s about the same size?

fifty five

If so, the writer **can imagine and then develop systems** that function to complete some purpose.

Look again at the *f*s.
Are the *f*s composed of a straight vertical line with a bar crossing in the center?

of thee I sing

If so, **orderliness** is evident, with **minimal imagination.**

Look at the entire writing samples.
Are there any hooks at the *beginning* of some or all letters? (Hooks can be located inside some letters as well.)

cat's in the cradle

If so, the writer wants to **own and possess** objects, people, or power. Neil Simon, the playwright, Princess Diana, David Letterman, Lee Iacocca, Dan Quayle, and O. J. Simpson exhibit multiple hooks. The writing of Jacqueline Kennedy Onassis and Brooke Shields contain relatively few hooks.

Look at the writing in both samples.

Are there hooks at the *end* of any letters?

Send the report

If so, the writer will hold on tightly to beliefs, possessions, friends. The more hooks, the more **tenacious** the writer.

Look at the *i*s in the samples.

Are the *i*s closely dotted near the stem?

Mississippi

If so, the writer pays **close attention to details** and often possesses a **good memory**.

Look at the strokes descending from the baseline in the *y*s, *g*s, and *j*s.

Are these strokes vertical without much curve in any direction (with or without loops)?

y g j q y

If so, the writer is determined to **follow through** with whatever is started. Such people usually do what they say they will do. Publisher Malcolm Forbes had remarkable follow-through.

Look at the bars of the *t* throughout the writing. Are the *t* bars strong and firm?

T'is Tell Tall Tales

If so, the writer is a good **self-starter** and can get projects going without being pushed.

Look at the lowercase *e*s in both samples. Are the loops open and wide?

feel the heat

If so, the writer is **receptive** to ideas that promote change and generally will seek out and explore different points of view, types of people, and new situations.

Are the *e* loops narrow, entirely closed, or muddied?

feel the heat

If so, the writer tends to be a **traditionalist** who prefers the "tried and true" and rejects ideas of change. He or she has a tendency to prejudge based on less than the latest information.

Look at the *t* bars in both samples.
Are some or all of them located on the left side of the *t* stem?

Britain procrastinates

If so, the writer has a tendency to put things off, to **procrastinate.**

Look at the endings of letters in the sample.
Are the endings made with firm, strong strokes?

firm and strong strokes

If so, the writer has the **ability to form clear opinions and act on them.**

Do the endings of letters, if any, fade or feather away?

green with fear

If so, a **fearfulness** is indicated and **indecisiveness** is likely. The writer tends to vacillate, yields easily to others, is reluctant to engage in any situation where decision making is critical.

Look at the lowercase *s*s.
Is the bottom stroke "soft," rounded, or feathery?

Soft strokes

If so, the writer **tends to cave in** to the forcefulness of others even if he or she has distinctly conflicting opinions. The writing of John Hinkley, who shot President Ronald Reagan, has soft *s*s.

Look at the entire writing sample, *including the* t *bars.*

Is there an upward slant of the letters or the *t* bars, or both?

> *Out of Africa has always meant more to watched my children responding to the fables son started to make African drawings,*

If so, the writer looks at the brighter side of life, **approaches problems with the opinion that they can be solved.** In the midst of mundane difficulties, this person's spirit still soars.

Look at the lowercase *m*s, *n*s, and *r*s in the samples.

Do any of the *r*s have flat tops, and do the *m*s and *n*s have rounded tops resembling those in the following illustration?

> *mutton roast*

If so, there is evidence of **manual dexterity,** a talent in plastic arts, an enjoyment and ability to productively use one's hands. Harry Houdini, the magician, had flat-topped *r*s.

Look at the *d*s, *e*s, and *r*s in the samples.
Do any of them resemble the illustrated letters?

> ∂ ε ɼ Ɛ

If so, the writer is likely to express ideas easily in writing or verbally. He or she may enjoy writing, literature, and other communicative arts. Babe Ruth, the baseball player, had a very well defined "Greek *e*," and so do Erica Jong, the writer, Mrs. Dwight D. (Mamie) Eisenhower, and Ingrid Bergman, the actress.

Look at the *"flow"* of both writing samples.
Is the flow even, with few corrections or erasures?

her prescience of how man would only hope was to get in tune with the movements of today, ecology,

If so, the writer thinks in a **steady** and **pleasingly consistent** way. Benjamin Franklin had extraordinary fluidity in his script, and so did Babe Ruth.

Look at the *t*s and *d*s in the samples.
Are the upstrokes retraced?

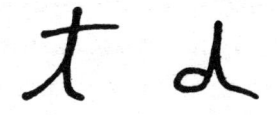

t d

If so, the writer feels that he or she **deserves respect** and may behave in what to others seems a **formal and dignified** manner.

Look at the dots over the *i*s or the *j*s in both samples.
Are the dots round and placed directly over the *i* or *j*? (The dots should be round but not circles.)

i i j

If so, **loyalty** and **faithfulness** are indicated. This may express itself toward a person, a principle, an abstract belief. Martin Luther King, Jr., had round dots.

Look again at the *i* or *j* dots.
Are they in the form of circles?

which one of his pickups went in the ditch?

If so, this represents **idiosyncratic, unconventional behavior.** While imagination is indicated, it usually manifests itself in the writer seeking ways to "be different." Interestingly, Jacquelyn Kennedy Onassis had circle-*i* dots.

Look at all the entire writing in both samples.
Do the letters lack beginning "approach" strokes?

[handwriting sample]

If so, this is evidence of **directness, straightforward thinking,** with little hesitation. John Lennon, the late Beatle, wrote like this.

Look at the lowercase *p*s in the samples.
Does the stem of the *p* begin at a point higher than that of the "buckle"?

[handwriting sample]

If so, this indicates an **insecure defensiveness** and a **tendency to argue.** If there is a loop on the buckle, the imagination is used to embellish arguments and defenses. If there is no loop, the writer argues mostly by marshaling facts.

Look at the *t* bars in the samples.
Do they make sweeping, energetic strokes across the stem?

[handwriting sample]

If so, it indicates **enthusiasm.** There is a **driving force** to accomplish goals. The more energy apparent in the *t* bar, the more powerful the writer's enthusiasm. Thomas Edison had energetic and sweeping *t* bars.

Look at the *i*s and *j*s in the samples.
Are the dots actually slashes? (These can be above or to either side of the letters.)

[Bill Clinton signature]

If so, this is a sign of **impatience, irritability.** Often indicates short-lived frustration. David Letterman slashes his dots.

Look at the *t*s and *d*s in the writing.

Are there any "tentlike" formations composed of straight lines?

The presiding

If so, it is a sign that the writer may **stubbornly resist changing opinions** even when it is realized that he or she may be in error. This is actually a fear trait—the **fear of losing face**. Luciano Pavarotti, the opera singer, makes tent formations.

Look at the strokes at the end of each word.

Are these strokes in the form of lengthened straight lines? Are there dashes throughout?

I have reached the

If so, this indicates someone who is **cautious** when it comes to taking risks. An excessive amount of such strokes indicates a limiting factor in the writer's life because the risk-taking level is so very low that most **opportunities are missed**. It also can signal a person who checks impulsive urges to control hurtful behavior with prudence. President Harry Truman's wife, Bess, had such writing.

Look at the *letter endings* throughout the samples.
Are the final strokes both long and turned slightly upward?

'twas The night before

If so, this indicates **generosity**. The writer is someone who gives and shares, without ulterior motive, and enjoys it.

Look again at the *letter endings*.
Are they long and curved upward in a flaunting way throughout?

for "yours"

If so, the writer **seeks attention and/or affection** in the form of praise, open admiration, encouragement, applause. These people will go out of their way to get it. Vanna White is such a writer.

Look at the lowercase *o*s and *a*s in the samples.
Are there loops inside any of these letters on the *right* side?

loop-d-loop

If so, this is a clue to the writer's **sense of privacy**. The person does not expose, for others to see, many of his or her emotions. These types are apt to be trustworthy when it involves information called "top secret." CIA agents tend to have right-side loops. David Letterman does too.

Look at the capital *M*s and *N*s in the samples.
Are there initial flourishes that are elegant and understated?

Millions, None.

If so, look for a **sense of humor** in the writer. These flourishes also are a sign of a **forgiving nature** and the ability to maintain **healthy perspectives.**

Look at the **ends of words** (primarily *m*s and *n*s) throughout both samples.

Do the endings taper off without losing the letters' identity?

[signature: Bess N. Truman]

If so, the writer is probably skillful at getting things done without hurting people's feelings, is usually **tactful,** is not always frank. Bess Truman was a champion in this realm.

Look at the *k*s in the samples.
Are the buckles disproportionately large?

[signature: Keith]

If so, a sign of **defiance**—to power, authority, conflicting opinion. Keith Richards of the Rolling Stones has exaggerated *k* buckles.

Look at the *t*s and *d*s in the samples.

Are the stems short in relation tot he other smaller letters?

Ronald

If so, this indicates a person who reserves the right and is willing to "make up his or her own mind" *before* anyone else "tells him or her" what to think first. This is often called **"independent"** thinking. George Bush falls into this category.

Look at the downstrokes in the *y*s, *g*s, and *j*s. Are the strokes straight and made without any loops?

Thank you for taking

If so, the writer prefers to be **without the physical company** of other people. This trait is seldom admitted by its possessor. David Letterman has straight strokes that end in hooks—indicating the trait of a loner who, if he ever does find somebody to be "alone" with, may be acutely possessive. Jimmy Carter is a loner too, as is Barbara Bush.

Look at the downstrokes of the *g*s, *j*s, and *y*s.

Are they strong and straight, with or without loops?

If so, this indicates **follow-through**. The stronger and straighter those strokes, the higher the **force of determination**. Malcolm Forbes had enormous determination, as did Sigmund Freud.

Look at the *t* stems and *d* stems in the samples. Are there loops in the stems?

If so, the writer's **feelings may be hurt easily**. The larger the loops, the more sensitive to criticism and harsh words. This trait is linked to imagination, and the writer may inflate and distort what others say.

Look at the *a*s and *o*s in the samples.
Are the tops of the letters open?

If so, the writer **likes to talk.** Former Secretary of State Alexander Haig, an acute open-looper, loved to talk and talk and talk. Greta Garbo, the *"I vant to be a lawn"* film actress, loved to talk, and she also would discipline herself to listen.

Look again at the *a*s and *o*s in the samples. Are most of them closed tightly?

If so, talking is not much of a pleasure for the writer. Many such writers are **good listeners**, since they use less time talking. Prince Charles of England is among these.

Look at the lowercase *a*s and *o*s in the samples. Are there looped formations inside these letters on the *left?*

If so, this indicates that the writer **may try to deceive him or herself** about reality-based odds and outcomes. Such people might avoid facing day-to-day problems head-on. Instead they tend to develop their own scenario about what the true picture is and act on it as if it were actual. Mia Farrow, the actress, is a left-looper.

Look yet again at the *a*s and *o*s in the samples. Are the circle loops clean inside, without erasures?

Henry Moore

If so, this is a clue to a writer who is **forthright** and **plain spoken.** Jacqueline Kennedy Onassis's circle loops were impeccably clean, as were Greta Garbo's and British sculptor Henry Moore's.

Look one more time at the lowercase *a*s and *o*s.
Are there loops inside the letters on *both* sides?

If so, these writers will deceive themselves and

then intentionally deceive others with altered facts, tall tales, and fraudulent epics. John Paul Jones, the American military leader, was a dedicated double-looper.

Look at the *t* bars in the samples.

Are there bars that do not go through the stem and are placed on the *right side?*

doing it well.!

If so, this can be a clue to **outbursts of emotion,** most often **anger.**

Look for a *short, straight line at the beginning* of any word.

This stroke also indicates **"temper."** The more of these "tic strokes" that are visible, the more likely these pent-up, uncontrolled episodes. Barbara Bush's *t* bars *fly* to the right side. Albert Einstein had multiple temper tics.

Look at the *writing* in both samples.
Do you see rigidly straight initial strokes from the baseline or below?

If so, the writer could be signaling **resentment**. Such writers may express annoyance and anger when anything they value is "intruded" upon. They strongly dislike someone *imposing* on them. This is based on their fear of being taken over by another mind. Albert Einstein often used rigid initial strokes.

Look at the *t* bars throughout both samples.
Does one end taper off into a fine needle point?

If so, the writer may use **cutting words to wound** others. Sarcasm may barely conceal anger and occasionally sadism. Walter Mondale, U.S. Ambassador to Japan, is among such writers. The ambassador's intense desire to acquire, combined with diplomatic talents, would blunt his sarcasm.

Look at the *last letters* of the words in both samples.

Do the final strokes or formations go back to the left?

[handwriting sample: Martina Navratilova]

If so, the writer tends to **blame him- or herself** for things that have happened in the past. (Combined with the needle points of sarcasm, the writer might inflict painful self-damage.) Tennis champion Martina Navratilova exhibits this formation.

Look at all the *capital letter beginning strokes.*

Are there small, flattened loops at the beginning of an initial downstroke?

[handwriting sample: Hand me the yogurt]

If so, there is **a fear of rivalry**. This **jealousy** might be kindled by the actual or imagined threat to a possession, friend, loved one, prestige, or power—whatever the writer feels rightfully belongs to him or her.

Look at the upstrokes and downstrokes of the *y*s, *g*s, and *j*s.
Do any of these strokes descend or rise to and become entangled with the lines above or below?

If so, this **confusion** indicates **scattered concentration**, often because of overloading of the mind with too many projects based on the level of ability to accomplish them. Dan Quayle and Marilyn Monroe entangle strokes.

Look at the *t* bars again.
Are they made with a forward and *downward* motion?

Great

If so, the writer tries to manage by a **dominating force of mind.** This is sometimes called "an air of command." At the extreme this trait becomes bullylike. The writing of former Governor Jerry Brown of California exhibits this.

Look at the *t* stems and *d* stems.
Are they at least 2.5 times as high as the mundane formations of the lowercase letters?

Sadat

If so, there is evidence of one who takes **exaggerated pride in oneself.** Henry Ford's writing gave clear indication of **vanity.**

Look at the *downstrokes* of gs, ys, and js as they descend beneath the baseline.
Are they exceedingly heavy and blunt?

If so, the writer **wishes to get credit without doing the job first.**

Look at the *signatures.*
Do the final strokes of the name develop into an *underscoring* feature?

Joan Crawford

If so, the writer enjoys **accomplishing tasks without help,** or with a minimum of assistance. Bob Hope shows self-reliance, as does actress Bette Midler and Fidel Castro. So did writer Edgar Allen Poe, founding father Benjamin Franklin, Houdini, and Napoleon.

Sexual Strokes

Earlier we looked at the lower loops, or the lack of them. However, at that time we did not consider sexuality.

Now look at the *"descenders"—the below-the-baseline downstrokes*—in both samples.

Are there long lower loops of proportionate size formed with a final stroke that comes *back up to the baseline*? (However, the descender must not slant to the right.)

If so, there is evidence of a **passionate nature**, an interest in lovemaking. This is an indication of **healthy desires** and ways to fulfill them. Actress Elizabeth Taylor has passionate loops, as did John F. Kennedy.

Look again.
Are the lower loops exaggeratedly large in relation to the rest of the writing?

If so, this indicates a preoccupation with sex and a **fantasy-filled sex life** that rarely achieves the poignancy of dreams.

Examine the *descenders*.

Are there long lower loops that *fail to return as high as the baseline?*

My dog has fleas

If so, this indicates an interest and ability to engage in sexual activity, yet the **desire may fade away** before physical involvement gets very far. Albert Einstein, who was not fond of "unnecessary emotional distraction," had such stopped-short loops.

Again, examine the *descenders*.

Are the loops narrow and squeezed? (The loops may, however, finish above the baseline.)

"yes, yes, yes," she yelped

If so, this indicates **sexual shyness, inhibition**. The writer can enjoy sexual pleasure if he or she can ever get to the point of trusting a partner. Handwriting that, in general, leans to the left accentuates the shy/inhibited trait. This person is seldom open to experimentation.

Look again at the *descenders*.
Is there a variety of lower loops in the same handwriting?

y g f y q

If so, the writer may **experiment rather freely in the erotic area** with an enjoyment of unusual, not necessarily "kinky," sexual practices.

Look again at the *descenders*.
Are there no lower loops at all?

for the future as highly appears

If so, this indicates a person who sees sexuality as a **down-to-earth practical function** that doesn't necessarily involve imagination or excessive emotion. He or she may be reliably monogamous. Actress Ingrid Bergman wrote without lower loops.

Once more examine the *descenders.*

Are there peculiar, oddly shaped loops, perhaps going in reverse-from-ordinary directions?

If so, these are indications of **sexual behavior that is so far beyond ordinary** that few others besides the writer may wish even to know about it.

Reexamine the *descenders.*

Do any of the lower loops drop so far below the baseline as to become inevitably entangled in the words of the line below?

If so, writers like this are compelled by **very strong sexual desires** that may tend to bring on confusion and lack of self-control. Their sexual fantasies may overwhelm them and others. They may seek to participate in orgiastic events.

Finally, examine the *descenders* again.

Are the descenders—straight or with a loop—relatively short?

If so, there is a tendency to avoid sexual actions or simply a **lack of interest in sexuality**. Joseph Stalin's descenders were short and stubby.

Compatibility

Now you have both columns in your notebook completed.

In some cases both you and your partner will share the same clues. Now it is time to make some comparisons.

Slant

BOTH WRITINGS SLANT IN THE SAME DIRECTION. You are likely to understand each other in the emotional realm. That helps in communication with one another.

BOTH HANDWRITINGS SLANT LEFT. There is likely to be less communication on virtually all levels. Occasional left-slanted pairings get along famously in bed.

BOTH SLANT RIGHT, NOT ALWAYS TO THE SAME DEGREE. There is a sympathy to one another's needs, both physical and emotional. Most people seem to slant slightly to the right.

ONE SLANTS RIGHT, THE OTHER SLANTS LEFT. There may never be full communication and understanding, and often frustration and irritation develop. The right-slanter wishes to share emotions with the left-slanter, who often keeps emotional experiences and other intimate feelings bottled up.

(A good example of non-compatibility in this area is former President Ronald Reagan and former Secretary of State Alexander Haig. The president's handwriting leaned slightly left—a man who rarely let his heart rule his head, even if he pretended at times to do so. General Haig's handwriting, on the other hand, leaned almost hysterically to the right.)

We did all that could

Ronald Reagan

and reminiscing.

Alexander Haig

Pressure

BOTH ARE LIGHT PRESSURE. The relationship is likely to be easygoing. The pair will get over disagreements and other bad moments swiftly and go on to something else. There is little grudge holding between the two.

Anthony Quinn

Nancy Reagan

BOTH ARE HEAVY PRESSURE. Tension and anxiety may pair with one another in such a relationship, which will be stormy at best. The people may share strong drives toward pleasure. *If they get there together,* the union can be sensational.

Carol Burnett

BOTH HEAVY PRESSURES SLANT IN OPPOSITE DIRECTIONS. The left-leaner is a pent-up volcano, the right-leaner is a powerful waterfall.

Edith Head

[signature]

Jesse Jackson

ONE IS MODERATE PRESSURE, THE OTHER HEAVY. The one with moderate-pressure may act as a safety valve for the other—if he or she can tolerate the strain.

To see a World in a Grain of Sand

William Blake

With all Good Wishes

Jeane Dixon

ONE IS MODERATE PRESSURE, ONE IS LIGHT. The moderate-pressure writer may propel the other into interesting circumstances. The light-pressure writer may relieve some of the moderate's moderate stress.

[signature]

Steve Martin

[signature]

Napoleon Bonaparte

Thinking Patterns

BOTH SHOW ROUNDED TOPS OF MS AND NS. Both take their time and don't rush themselves or others. They think things through before they blow their top, which they don't often do. They are the kind of sexual animals who play Ravel's *Bolero* at bedtime.

men are created

Brooke Shields

John Adams

John Adams

ONE ROUNDED, ONE WITH NEEDLE POINTS. This pairs a methodical, logical thinker who requires a relatively long time to come to a conclusion with a fast calculator to whom the answers come quickly. The faster thinker may find his or her patience tried. The methodical thinker may feel uncomfortable at being considered somewhat "slow." The faster thinker almost always must give way in this pairing, because the slower thinker can't "speed up." And even then, they often don't mesh.

BOTH WITH NEEDLE POINTS. Two very quick thinkers. Needle points often are a sign of original minds. When combined with healthy lower loops, this can produce a wealth of fascinating ideas.

Donald Trump

Barry Goldwater

NOTE: "**Mountain peaks**" get along well with almost anybody because they think faster than rounders, although not as fast as needle points. Mountaintops are investigative and often can bring things to the table for the needle points to decide about quickly, and the rounders to mull over.

General Manuel Antonio Noriega

NOTE: **Breaks between letters,** the signs of **intuitive process,** speeds up all thinking. People with both needle points and breaks between letters are unusual thinkers. Rounders with breaks between letters think much faster than regular rounders.

one country, one

Frederick Douglass

Size

BOTH WITH SMALL-SIZE LETTERS. These people display heavy-duty concentration on what they do together and separately. A trait such as a temper or a curious mind, for example, will be magnified and intensified.

ONE WITH SMALL LETTERS AND ONE WITH LARGE. While the large writer demands space to express ideas freely, the small writer can make love on the edge of a sword. Small writers often are "completers" of projects, while large writers may leave them partially undone. A couple with this combination will have many petty annoyances and irritations with one another that may, unless they also are both tactful, result in a split.

MIDDLING LETTERS. This is what most of us are, adjustable.

BOTH WITH LARGE LETTERS. Reality takes a beating with such a pair. Their worlds will be almost as expansive as their egos, which interfere with their understanding. Few others could stay sane for long in the same room with them. They each ought to sleep in a double king bed.

Clarity vs. *Muddiness*

BOTH WITH CLEAR WRITING. Fine.

Sugar Ray Robinson

Ingrid Bergman

ONE WITH CLEAR AND ONE WITH MUDDY WRITING. The clear writer will soon become troubled with the excesses of the other.

BOTH WITH MUDDY WRITING. Excessive in almost every way.

J Paul Getty

J. Paul Getty

I am happy to be

Senator Hubert Humphrey

Imagination

Imagination encompasses friendship, change and variety, creativity, and the ability to originate novel ideas.

BOTH WITH MIDDLE-SIZE LOWER LOOPS. This pair probably will get along in a middling sort of way and enjoy many of the same stimuli.

ONE WITH NO LOOPS, ONE WITH BIG LOOPS. A solitary soul and a free spirit. A "factual" thinker who loves routine paired with a person who detests routine and adds imaginative ideas and perspectives to the fabric of truth. There is potential for falling in love here.

Aristotle Onassis

Judy Garland

BOTH WITH NO LOOPS. These people inhabit "real" worlds with "real" problems and "real" solutions that can be described in numbers and symbols. They remain steadfastly immune to imagination and exaggeration. Passion is possible with great expenditures of energy.

Philosophical

BOTH WITH LARGE UPPER LOOPS. These people get a kick out of mind games, and they play them with each other. They are frequently found in churches and other places of worship.

John Belushi

Walt Disney

One with large upper loops, one with no loops or short loops. One with a mystical sense and one without. The large looper will try to get the no-looper to soar into the worlds beyond, and the no-looper or short-looper will doubt it can be done.

Goals

BOTH WITH FLYING *T* BARS. This pair may share visions of the future that are far beyond their ability to reach. Only if their drives to achieve are extraordinary will they get to their shared dreams. This is a long-shot pairing that can be historic if it succeeds.

ONE WITH FLYING *T* BARS, ONE WITH LOW *T* BARS. One overestimates his or her own ability to achieve, and the other underestimates it. The optimism of the flying *t* might kill the low *t*.

BOTH WITH HIGH *T* BARS. These two are ambitious in the most practical ways, for themselves and each other.

BOTH WITH LOW *T* BARS. This pair fears they cannot dream up a future and then make it happen. Often they are correct.

BOTH WITH *T* BARS ALL OVER THE PLACE. Their goals are inconsistent. They search yet seldom steer for long in any one direction. They yearn for a balanced place to settle down between no goals and unrealistic ones.

NOTE: **Basin bars** are drawn by people who will not project themselves far enough into the future to become wedded to a long-term goal, including a lasting personal relationship. They are short-termers in most ways.

Achievement

BOTH WITH TIE STROKES. This pair goes through muck and mire, thick and thin, rejection and humiliation, and keeps on trucking.

Vladimir Horowitz

Fidel Castro

ONE WITH TIE STROKES AND ONE WITHOUT. These two may be especially helpful in a business relationship.

BOTH WITHOUT TIE STROKES. The problem here is a double disinterest in pursuit without external instigation and encouragement. In business this pairing is slow death.

BOTH WITH BREAKAWAY STROKES. They usually see a chance to take action before others see it, and they'll go for it. This combination can have profit and fun.

No breakaway strokes. This pair may see no need for action to alter the status quo.

One with breakaways, one without. One sees and acts on opportunities early, and it's possible the other will enjoy the adventure.

Aggression

Both with below-the-line breakaways. These two people are energetic and forceful when they go after something.

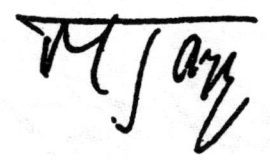

Mick Jagger

Beethoven

BOTH WITHOUT BREAKAWAYS. If the energy and force isn't there, neither seems to miss it.

ONE WITH BREAKAWAYS, ONE WITH NO BREAKAWAYS. There may be uncomfortable times when one pursues hotly while the other can't get the afterburners lighted.

BOTH WITH TALL *D*S AND *T*S. They want respect from one another because each feels worthy of respect in dress, manner, and intellect.

If pride turns to vanity in one of the pair, he or she may experience feelings of jealousy about the other's stronger confidence.

[signature]

Dr. Martin Luther King

[signature]

Bruce Springsteen

BOTH WITHOUT TALL *D*S AND *T*S. They are fearful about their self-image, and they show this to one another.

ONE WITH TALL *D*S AND *T*S, AND ONE WITHOUT. The one who thinks most of herself or himself may try to "go along" with the other's low "self-esteem." But the one with the low self-opinion is likely to feel inferior in this relationship.

Organizational Ability

BOTH WITH EQUAL *F* LOOPS. This indicates two people with organizational ability, orderliness, and good imagination, a good business combination. These people have moments in bed.

BOTH WITH NO *F* LOOPS AT ALL. A neat and orderly pair. They go by the book.

ONE WITH EQUAL *F* LOOPS AND ONE WITH NO *F* LOOPS. One enjoys what the other brings neatly to the table.

Possession

BOTH WITH INITIAL HOOKS. They may go out of their way to own or possess things they desire. This pair is like living Velcro.

O. J. Simpson

Princess Diana

BOTH WITHOUT ANY HOOKS AT ALL. They are easy-come, easy-go about possessions and exhibit no driving need to get more.

ONE WITH HOOKS, ONE WITH NO HOOKS. "Hooks" eventually may see "no hooks" as one who "does not share the load." "No hooks" may resent "hooks'" priorities, which ranks "having" higher than appreciating or enjoying.

Tenacity

BOTH WITH ENDING HOOKS. They may not be able to throw away anything. Their house and offices may become trash cluttered, just like the rest of their life. They can become utterly entangled. The more hooks, the harder it will be to let each other or anything else go.

BOTH WITH NO ENDING HOOKS AT ALL. They don't hold on to much for very long. They may have the desire to acquire but not necessarily to keep. This could bode ill for a business or personal relationship.

ONE WITH ENDING HOOKS AND ONE WITHOUT. The one with hooks may seem oppressively possessive to the one without.

Details and Memory

BOTH WITH CLOSELY DOTTED *I*S. This pair pays attention to each other's birthdays, gets the bills paid on time.

This is my story both humble and true
Take it to pieces and mend it with glue.

John Lennon

Houdini

Harry Houdini

BOTH WITH NO *I* DOTS. They will forget crucial details and their life together may become a mess.

ONE WITH AND ONE WITHOUT *I* DOTS. They may become "the Odd Couple."

Follow-Through

BOTH WITH STRONG, STRAIGHT DOWNSTROKES. This pair will do what they say they will do and thus will learn to rely on each other's word. Projects they undertake are likely to be completed.

BOTH WITH CURVED OR FADING DOWNSTROKES. They'll take a swing at things but almost always pull up short.

ONE WITH STRONG, STRAIGHT DOWNSTROKES AND THE OTHER WITH CURVED, FADING DOWNSTROKES. In a partnership, this combination becomes annoying and doubles the load on the straight, firm downstroker.

Drive

BOTH WITH STRONG, FIRM *T* BARS. This pair enjoys a high energy level that needs no jump-starting to get going. Both can initiate powerful experiences, sometimes at the same time.

BOTH WITHOUT STRONG, FIRM *T* BARS. This pair waits to be pushed to get something important going.

ONE WITH AND ONE WITHOUT FIRM, STRONG *T* BARS. Such a couple will display an imbalance of power that eventually will cause strains and rifts.

Mindedness

BOTH WITH WIDE, OPEN *E* LOOPS. This pair is willing to enter each other's world and accept the differences there.

*Dear Incognito:
we must get together
next year. ам*

Ernest Hemingway

Liberace

BOTH WITH CLOSED *E* LOOPS. Each lives alone in his or her own world and wants no intrusions or other reasons for change. Both refuse to see more than they can understand. Some call this "tunnel vision." A full range of sensuality is never open to such people, and that's how they prefer it.

ONE WITH CLOSED, ONE WITH OPEN *E* LOOPS. In this pair, the closed one may fear that the open one is running off the track. This is a very common pairing in modern American marriage and business partnerships. Disharmony is almost a sure thing.

Procrastination

BOTH WITH *T* BARS ON THE LEFT SIDE OF *T* STEM. This pair puts off almost everything for tomorrow and the tomorrow after that. Both fear the future. One often picks on the other for putting things off.

ONE *T* BAR THROUGH THE STEM AND ONE TO THE LEFT. One has drive and energy to get going on something, and the other hangs back reluctantly, fearful of consequences. In this relationship there will be many headaches at night.

BOTH WITH *T* BARS THROUGH THE STEM. Both have willpower.

Decision Making

BOTH WITH FIRM, STRONG FINAL STROKES. This pair forms individual opinions and holds them independently of each other. Neither is tentative about making decisions.

Frank Sinatra

> by the peoples, for the peoples, shall not per-
> ish from the earth.
>
> Abraham Lincoln
> November 19, 1863.

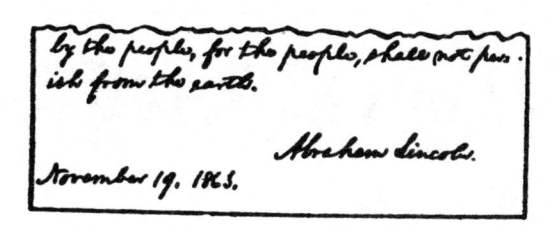

Abraham Lincoln

BOTH WITH FADED FINAL STROKES. Neither one dares to do much for fear of failure. This is not a partnership favored by high achievers or lovers.

ONE WITH FIRM FINAL STROKES AND ONE WITH FADED. This relationship of leader and follower can work to the advantage of both. However, if faded unfades, a modern melodrama of power and usurpation often ensues.

Stance

BOTH WITH SMALL, SOFT *S* STROKES. This pair will not stand firm. Each one can be profoundly influenced by others, and all their firmest convictions yield to superior persuasion.

[signature]

Bill Clinton

[signature]

General Manuel Noriega

BOTH HAVE *S* STROKES THAT COME FORWARD. This pair will "stick by its guns."

ONE WITH SOFT *S* STROKES AND ONE WITH FIRM FORWARD S STROKES. In a partnership this can be a flexible success, as long as it lasts. People who hold loyalty in the highest regard should avoid this pairing.

[signature: Trusting this note is satisfactory,]

President Gerald Ford

This is probably typical of my various handwritings!

Dr. Karl Menninger

Frame of Mind

BOTH WITH UPWARD-SLANTING LETTERS. This pair sees the manure and asks, "Where's the pony?" They feel good about life and go toward the future. Past for them is prologue. Their lack of negativism gives them an excellent chance at reaching the goals they set.

*Cordially,
Lou Gehrig*

Lou Gehrig

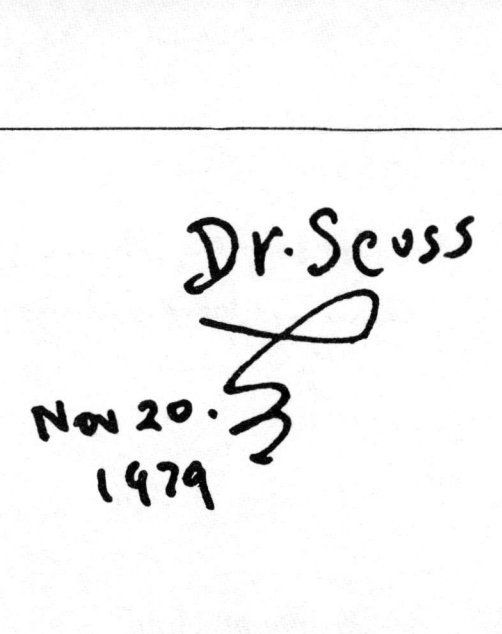

Dr. Seuss

BOTH WITH DOWNWARD-DROOPING LETTERS. For them, the swimming pool is always half empty. They say *"No, no, no!"* if they reach a sexual climax. In the business world they would be Gloom & Doom.

Manual Dexterity

BOTH WITH FLAT-TOP *R*S **AND/OR ROUNDED** *M*S **AND** *N*S. This pair is doubly handy almost anywhere. They can make and fix things with precision and speed. People who are good with their hands often feel kinship with others similarly endowed.

[signature: Th Jefferson]

Thomas Jefferson

[signature: A. Graham Bell.]

Alexander Graham Bell

ONE WITH FLAT-TOP *R*S AND/OR ROUNDED *M*S AND *N*S AND ONE WITHOUT. The one without handiness may well appreciate the one with it.

BOTH WITHOUT. In order for this pairing to work, a terrific sense of humor is required.

Symbol Manipulation

BOTH HAVE GREEK *E*S AND *R*S AND/OR DELTA *D*S. This pair may enjoy working the London *Times* crossword puzzles. They both love to throw words and other symbols back and forth.

ONE WITH GREEK *E*S AND *R*S AND/OR DELTA *D*S AND ONE WITHOUT. One lives by reason, the other by wits. This can be a useful combination.

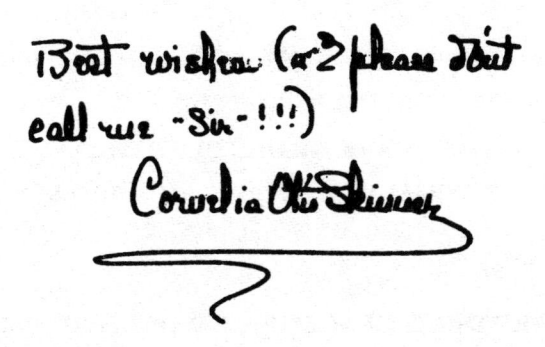

Best wishes (or 2 please don't call me "Sir"!!!)
Cornelia Otis Skinner

Cornelia Otis Skinner

Best Wishes

Donald Trump

BOTH WITHOUT GREEK *ES* AND *RS* AND/OR DELTA *D*S. This pair may be called "unaffected," since most of what they know was learned from first-hand experience rather than teaching.

Flow

BOTH WRITINGS ARE GRACEFUL WITH FEW CORRECTIONS OR ERASURES. This pair moves well together.

ONE WRITING IS GRACEFUL AND ONE, ARRHYTHMIC. They will bump into one another and step on each other's toes. Another combination that can be saved by a sense of humor.

I told my husband about your wonderful program!

Barbara Bush

support — Bar sends her love — gratefully, GB

George Bush

BOTH ARRHYTHMIC. This pairing may be comical, or it may be heartbreaking.

Self-Image

BOTH WITH RETRACED *T*S AND *D*S. This pair adheres to certain standards for image and are uncomfortable unless these standards are met.

ONE WITH RETRACED *T*S AND *D*S AND ONE WITHOUT. One may disapprove of the conduct, dress or language of the other, and also will be easily offended by undignified situations.

BOTH WITHOUT RETRACED *T*S AND *D*S. This pair may go off in directions unapproved by anyone.

Salvador Dali

Harry S Truman

Bonding

BOTH WITH ROUND DOTS OVER *I*S AND *J*S. This pair forms long, strong bonds with people, values, and beliefs.

ONE WITH ROUND DOTS OVER *I*S AND *J*S, THE OTHER WITHOUT. One feels bonded, the other feels unbound.

BOTH WITHOUT ROUND DOTS OVER THE *I*S AND *J*S. Neither bonds easily, and their relationship may slip rather easily.

Idiosyncrasies

BOTH HAVE ROUND CIRCLES OVER *I*S AND *J*S. Each has a deliberate desire to be outstanding in an individual and possibly unconventional way.

they desire

Michael Jackson

love, Richard

Richard Simmons

ONE WITH CIRCLES, ONE WITHOUT. One strives to be different, the other is satisfied not to be. This combination commonly works—unless the striving quality is obnoxiously exaggerated.

BOTH WITHOUT CIRCLES. Commonplace.

Simplicity

BOTH WITHOUT BEGINNING APPROACH STROKES. These two don't waste time with windups and hesitations. They strip away the unnecessary. Their thinking is uncomplicated and can be elegant. In business, science, art and music, these two are almost always a good mesh.

Henry Moore

Henry Moore

[handwritten text by William Faulkner]

William Faulkner

ONE WITH APPROACH STROKES, ONE WITHOUT. This combination gets places by a more circuitous route.

BOTH WITH APPROACH STROKES. They tend to beat around the bush.

Fighting Spirit

BOTH WITH *P* STEM BEGINNING HIGHER THAN *P* BUCKLE. This pair fights anybody, including each other.

Al Capone

Zsa Zsa Gabor

ONE WITH HIGH *P* STEM, THE OTHER WITHOUT. This pair is comically depicted in many sitcoms. It is actually quite a common pairing.

BOTH WITHOUT HIGH *P* STEMS. Their dander is not raised easily.

Enthusiasm

BOTH HAVE SWEEPING *T* BARS. This pair eagerly goes after what it desires. The energy this combination expends goes beyond what is needed to accomplish a goal or purpose. This excess energy often insures achievement. In the business world, enthusiasm is almost always the hallmark of success.

I'm walking down the street to get

Hugh Hefner

With Best Wishes
Martin Luther King Jr.

Dr. Martin Luther King

ONE WITH SWEEPING *T* BARS, ONE WITHOUT. This pair expresses limited passion.

BOTH WITHOUT SWEEPING *T* BARS. This pair represses most eagerness with fearfulness.

Irritability

BOTH WITH SLASHED *I* AND *J* DOTS. This pair may be frustrated by anything that slows their pace. Frustration adds heavily to mutual stress, which in this pair may be high.

David Letterman

Dan Quayle

ONE WITH SLASHED *I* AND *J* DOTS, THE OTHER WITHOUT. In business, this pair may work well, provided the *non*slasher is willing to put up with bouts of frustrated huffing and puffing.

BOTH WITHOUT SLASHED *I* AND *J* DOTS. A detail-oriented pair with a good grasp of realities.

Persuadability

BOTH WITH RIGID, TENTLIKE STROKES IN *T*S AND *D*S. This pair sticks its collective heels in the dirt and will not be moved. They might each stand firm on shaky ground despite attempts to "reason" with them. They may fear loss of face and might be easily persuaded by flattery.

change Russia, but I am sure it will strengthen Russian Jewry

Yours
D. Ben-Gurion

David Ben-Gurion

Lord Snowden

ONE WITH RIGID, TENTLIKE STROKES, ONE WITHOUT. There will be many missed opportunities with this combination.

BOTH WITHOUT RIGID, TENTLIKE STROKES. A good bet in business and pleasure. They are willing to listen to one another and to others. They are not crushed if proven wrong.

Timing

BOTH WITH LONG, STRAIGHT, FINAL STROKES OR SEVERAL DASHES. This pair needs extra time to explore and reason before it makes a decisive move. Prudence is the watchword of people with this writing style.

[signature: Edith Roosevelt]

Mrs. Teddy Roosevelt

[signature: Helen H. Taft]

Mrs. William Howard Taft

ONE WITH LONG FINAL STROKES PLUS DASHES AND ONE WITHOUT. The one without may take the longer, safer way, while the other takes more chances. A frequent business partnership.

BOTH WITHOUT LONG FINAL STROKES. Fairly common combination that does little that is rash.

Generosity

BOTH WITH FINAL STROKES THAT ARE LONG AND TURN SLIGHTLY UPWARD. This pair is kind, seldom spiteful, and open-minded.

Billy Joel

Ella Fitzgerald

ONE WITH LONG, UPTURNED FINAL STROKES, THE OTHER WITHOUT. This can be nice, especially if the less generous one is able to accept generosity gracefully.

BOTH WITHOUT LONG, SLIGHTLY UPTURNED FINAL STROKES. With this pair, sharing is not always easy, and when one needs something the other has, that something may be denied.

Need for Attention

BOTH WITH LONG, ENTIRELY UPTURNED FINAL STROKES THAT ARE FLAUNTED THROUGHOUT THE WRITING. This pair demands affectionate attention from others and each other. If they don't get it, they may initiate obnoxious behavior to get attention.

Paul Gauguin

Vanna White

ONE WITH LONG, UPTURNED, FLAUNTED FINALS, ONE WITHOUT. This pair may work if the one who needs attention less gives generously of his or her warmth and affection to the other.

BOTH WITHOUT LONG, UPTURNED FINALS. Ordinary attention will do in this relationship.

Sense of Privacy

BOTH WITH LOOPS INSIDE ANY LOWERCASE *O*S OR *A*S ON THE RIGHT SIDE. This pair holds their individual cards close to their vests and may not share things, even with one another. Confidentiality is their watchword.

ONE WITH RIGHT LOOPS, ONE WITHOUT. One keeps secrets from the other. This may get annoying for the one secrets are kept from. Often the "secrets" are of little importance to others and are best if kept secret.

a wonderful, growing experience!

Oprah Winfrey

character but what he can prove, HiSTORy could

Michael Jackson

BOTH WITHOUT RIGHT LOOPS. There is minimal secrecy between the two, and most issues are brought quickly into the open. This can be a good business and personal combination.

Sense of Humor

BOTH WITH UNDERSTATED INITIAL LETTER FLOURISHES. This pair laughs at life and its interesting twists. Both usually are well liked by others, and they can find ways to get along truthfully with one another. Sex for them may be blissfully funny.

Marlo Thomas

Benjamin Franklin

ONE WITH FLOURISHES AND ONE WITHOUT. One tends to be forgiving to others and the self; the other is less so.

BOTH WITHOUT INITIAL FLOURISHES. In this relationship, "seriousness" is seldom relieved by truthful humor.

Tact

BOTH WITH TAPERING FINAL LETTERS THAT DO NOT LOSE FORM AND IDENTITY. This pair may have a relatively frictionless relationship based on skillful, mannerly handling of threatening situations. While they rarely are encountered together, they can be unusually successful at the negotiating table and in the bedchamber.

Pat Nixon

Bess Truman

ONE WITH TAPERING FINAL LETTERS, ONE WITHOUT. This offers a more peaceful combination than if neither one tapers off.

BOTH WITHOUT TAPERING FINAL LETTERS. These two people may sometimes indulge in the desire to hurt each other and the rest of the world, too.

Resistance and Refusal

BOTH WITH OVERSIZED K BUCKLES. This pair will bravely stand up and strike out against authority. Neither is easily intimidated by powerful threats.

NOTE: Another clue to defiance is an exaggerated letter, usually in the form of a capital within a word.

Merle Oberon

Don King

ONE WITH LARGE *K* BUCKLE, ONE WITHOUT. This pairing may be iffy unless the partner without *k* buckles has a lot of tact.

BOTH WITHOUT *K* BUCKLES. A tendency to eschew physical or intellectual violence.

Mind Control

BOTH WITH SHORT *T* AND *D* STEMS. This pair chooses to form individual conclusions. Sometimes they'll agree, sometimes not.

ONE WITH SHORT *T* AND *D* STEMS AND ONE WITHOUT. The one who chooses to make up his or her own mind may attempt to exert persuasive influence on the one who considers many other opinions before making a decision.

BOTH WITHOUT SHORT *T* AND *D* STEMS. This pair does not hesitate to consult.

ONE OR BOTH WITH A MIXTURE OF TALL AND SHORT *T* AND *D* STEMS. Nice balance between independent thought and willingness to consider the opinions of others.

Insularity

BOTH WITH STRAIGHT STROKES AND NO LOOPS. This pair prefer their own company to that of others. They are not happy socialites.

Sean Connery

Grace Kelly

ONE WITH STRAIGHT, LOOPLESS STROKES, THE OTHER WITH LOOPS. This pair can work if the more gregarious partner respects the loner's desire to be alone—and if the loner also comes out of the shell at times.

BOTH WITH LOOPS. This pair likes to meet and greet people. It's a promising match in a retail business.

Illusions

BOTH WITH INFLATED *D* AND *T* LOOPS. This pair could be headed for deflation because they both can be acutely concerned with what others think about them. They fear that others will not see them as they see themselves, and they don't want anybody puncturing their balloon.

Geraldo Rivera

Woody Allen

One with inflated *d* and *t* loops, one without. One will hate the pinprick of criticism and the other would do well not to criticize, when tact is better employed.

Both without inflated *d* and *t* loops. If somebody flings a pointed criticism, both will consider the source and perhaps deflect it with understanding.

Loquacity

Both with the tops of *a*s and *o*s open. This pair could, if the openings on top are wide enough, talk forty-eight hours each day. If they have moderate-size openings, they may stop talking in their sleep.

Mrs Haig and I send

Alexander Haig

the horse & carriage out of the old garage. Hugh M Hefner

Hugh Hefner

ONE WITH OPEN *O*S AND *A*S, AND ONE WITH CLOSED *O*S AND *A*S. This pair may work if one talks and the other listens. The listener may suffer frequent headaches.

BOTH WITH CLOSED *O*S AND *A*S. They will listen first, talk later. In the same room with one another, there may be lengthy silences.

Self-Deceit

BOTH WITH LOOPS ON LEFT-HAND SIDE OF *A*S AND *O*S. This pair reshapes reality to suit themselves and then acts upon it. This Quixotic trait can land them both in the soup or open up new worlds— but it is mostly treacherous for them and for their friends and lovers.

[signature: Leo Tolstoy]

Count Leo Tolstoy

[signature: Humphrey Bogart]

Humphrey Bogart

ONE WITH LEFT-SIDE LOOPS, ONE WITHOUT. One sees his or her individual reality, and the other sees things more as most people do. Hard in business, lonesome in pleasure.

BOTH WITHOUT LEFT-SIDE LOOPS. This pair shares a healthy respect for reality.

BOTH WITH *A*S AND *O*S THAT ARE CLEAN INSIDE. They communicate unmistakably and probably without treachery.

Cunning

BOTH HAVE LOOPS ON BOTH THE LEFT AND RIGHT INSIDE OF THE *A*S AND *O*S. This pair is doubly cunning. Sooner or later they may make a fool of the wrong person, and that can lead to violence.

John Paul Jones

Linda Evans

One with left and right loops, the other without loops. In certain professions this could be useful, but the loopless partner must make frequent reality checks.

Temper

Both with a *t* bar that doesn't go through the stem and is located on the right side. This pair carry pent-up fears that, when aroused, burst out into furious words and movements. This can get physically dangerous.

NOTE: **Temper tics** indicate the same tendency to outbursts as right-side *t* bars.

auch, wie systematisch dafür

Albert Einstein

I don't know what you're doing at Emery - but you're certainly doing it well!

Barbara Bush

ONE WITH RIGHT-SIDE *T* BARS OR TEMPER TICS, THE OTHER WITHOUT. Only with the utmost patience and understanding can a person without a temper live or work comfortably with right-side *t* bars and temper tics.

Stance

BOTH WITH STRAIGHT AND RIGID INITIAL UP-STROKES. This pair is easily insulted by people who invade their space, spend their time, share their possessions. Often they display showy resentment.

ONE WITH STRAIGHT, RIGID INITIAL UPSTROKES, ONE WITHOUT. Only respect for a "difficult" personality can keep this pairing from coming apart.

BOTH WITHOUT RIGID STROKES. This pair operates with a lack of resentment.

Sarcasm

BOTH WITH *T* BARS THAT TAPER OFF INTO FINE NEEDLE POINTS. This pair will brutally stab one another with words, and their "humor" is almost always at another's expense. Their patter is exceedingly tiresome to those who hate cruelty.

Tennessee Williams

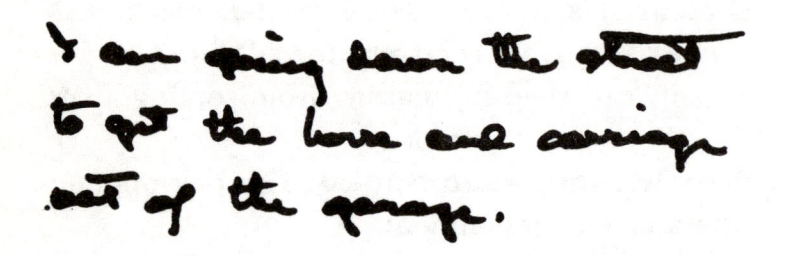

Senator Edmund Muskie

ONE WITH TAPERING NEEDLE-STROKE *T* BARS AND ONE WITHOUT. The one who is hurtful will keep it up until the other cries "enough."

Guilt

BOTH WITH FINAL STROKES OF LAST LETTERS IN A WORD GOING ALL THE WAY BACK TO THE LEFT. This pair can suffer memories of humiliation and shame that are vivid and fresh in their minds. They may shoulder the blame and berate themselves—not each other—for past actions, long after those actions no longer have real consequences. This pair can be manipulated by guilt-trip artists.

Desi Arnaz, Jr.

Jenny Lind

ONE WITH BACKWARD LEFT STROKES AND ONE WITHOUT. One takes the blame for the past and the other looks blamelessly toward the future.

Jealousy

BOTH WITH SMALL, FLATTENED LOOPS AT THE BEGINNING OF AN INITIAL DOWNSTROKE. This pair reacts strongly to any perceived threat to share what is "rightfully" theirs. They are ever vigilant to fight against another trying to take their position or fortune. Violence is a real possibility.

ONE WITH SMALL, FLATTENED LOOPS, THE OTHER WITHOUT. This pair gets along with difficulty. One may think he or she possesses the other and will battle furiously to keep intruders away.

Confusion

BOTH WITH ASCENDERS OR DESCENDERS THAT INTERMINGLE. This pair sacrifices precision and timing in order to enjoy variety. In business, it's a sloppy relationship that often results in sloppy work.

ONE WITH INTERMINGLING, THE OTHER WITHOUT. This pairing can be tedious and heartbreaking for both.

Dominance

BOTH WITH BLUNT-TIPPED *T* BARS THAT GO FORWARD AND DOWNWARD. This pair will take command and get things done. There can be trouble between them unless the order-giver also knows how to *take* orders. Dwight D. Eisenhower stands almost alone among recent public figures in this realm of dominance.

[signature]

Dwight Eisenhower

ONE WITH BLUNT, DOWNWARD *T* BARS AND ONE WITHOUT. The one without blunt, downward *t* bars may find him- or herself subservient to the other.

Vanity

BOTH WITH EXAGGERATEDLY TALL *T*S AND *D*S. Both members of this pair tend to preen.

[signature]

Teddy Kennedy

[signature: Fidel Castro]

Fidel Castro

ONE WITH EXAGGERATED *T*S AND *D*S AND THE OTHER WITHOUT EXAGGERATION. One must applaude him- or herself; the other must get used to it or split.

Bluff

BOTH WITH EXCEEDINGLY HEAVY AND BLUNT DOWNSTROKES OF *G*S, *Y*S, AND *J*S. This pair will lead others to believe they have something they don't.

[handwriting: What do you think of my]

Robert Kennedy

One with blunt, heavy downstrokes, one without. One uses an excess of energy to mask emptiness, and the other may worry that his or her partner's bluff will be called.

Self-Reliance

Both underscore their signature. This pair does things well independently. This can be a successful business combination.

Billy Graham

Stavros Niarchos

One underscored signature, one without. This combination works well.

BOTH WITHOUT UNDERSCORED SIGNATURES. Many people don't underscore.

The Sexual Loop Guide

BOTH WITH LONG LOWER LOOPS OF *G*S, *Y*S, AND *J*S THAT RETURN TO THE BASELINE. In lovemaking, this pair is likely to be active and play the "normal" sex roles.

Miles Standish

Priscilla Presley

BOTH WITH LONG LOWER LOOPS THAT FAIL TO RETURN TO THE BASELINE. This pair is willing to "make love," but they get to everything prematurely.

BOTH WITH NARROW, SQUEEZED LOWER LOOPS THAT RETURN TO THE BASELINE. This pair is sexually inhibited by fear of trusting.

ONE WITH EXAGGERATED, ODD, OR ENTANGLED LOWER LOOPS AND ONE WITH SQUEEZED LOOPS OR NONE. This pair is a mismatch and has little chance of communicating.

BOTH WITH A VARIETY OF LOWER LOOPS. This pair does a lot of sexual research and investigation that seldom extends beyond the merely unusual.

BOTH WITH NO LOWER LOOPS AT ALL. This pair treats human sexual activity as a simple reproductive function that can be made efficient and productive.

BOTH WITH STRANGE, ODDLY SHAPED LOOPS. This pair is beyond kinky.

BOTH WITH EXAGGERATED LOWER LOOPS IN RELATION TO REST OF WRITING. This pair finds its sexual satisfaction in fantasy, and neither may need the other to have fun.

Judy Garland

Mickey Rooney

BOTH WITH ENTANGLED LOWER LOOPS. This pair, led by fascination with genitalia, will not be wallflowers at the orgy.

BOTH WITH SHORT, STRAIGHT G, Y, AND J LOOPS. This pair would rather see a G-rated movie.